BALLADS
PLAYALONG SOLOS FOR FLUTE

Arrangements by Jack Long

HOW TO USE THE CD ACCOMPANIMENT:

A melody cue appears on the right channel only. If your CD player has a balance adjustment, you can adjust the volume of the melody by turning down the right channel.

ISBN 0-634-00448-4

HAL•LEONARD®
CORPORATION

7777 W. BLUEMOUND RD. P.O. BOX 13819 MILWAUKEE, WI 53213

Visit Hal Leonard Online at
www.halleonard.com

BRIDGE OVER TROUBLED WATER ◆

Flute

Words and Music by
PAUL SIMON

3

4

BRING HIM HOME 2
from LES MISÉRABLES

Flute

Music by CLAUDE-MICHEL SCHÖNBERG
Lyrics by HERBERT KRETZMER and ALAIN BOUBLIL

I DREAMED A DREAM

from LES MISÉRABLES

Music by CLAUDE-MICHEL SCHÖNBERG
Lyrics by HERBERT KRETZMER
Original Text by ALAIN BOUBLIL and JEAN-MARC NATEL

Flute

CANDLE IN THE WIND ◆④

Music by ELTON JOHN
Words by BERNIE TAUPIN

Flute

DON'T CRY FOR ME ARGENTINA 5

from EVITA

Words by TIM RICE
Music by ANDREW LLOYD WEBBER

Flute

MCA MUSIC PUBLISHING

I DON'T KNOW HOW TO LOVE HIM 6

from JESUS CHRIST SUPERSTAR

Flute

Words by TIM RICE
Music by ANDREW LLOYD WEBBER

MCA MUSIC PUBLISHING

I KNOW HIM SO WELL 7
from CHESS

Words and Music by BENNY ANDERSSON,
TIM RICE and BJORN ULVAEUS

Flute

dim.

IMAGINE

Flute

Words and Music by
JOHN LENNON

Medium slow (♩ = 76)

KILLING ME SOFTLY WITH HIS SONG ◆ 9

Words by NORMAN GIMBEL
Music by CHARLES FOX

FLUTE

NIGHTS IN WHITE SATIN ◆10

Words and Music by
JUSTIN HAYWOOD

Flute

ONE DAY I'LL FLY AWAY

Flute

Words and Music by
JOE SAMPLE and WILL JENNINGS

WONDERFUL TONIGHT

FLUTE

Words and Music by
ERIC CLAPTON

PLAY MORE OF YOUR FAVORITE SONGS
WITH GREAT INSTRUMENTAL FOLIOS FROM HAL LEONARD

Best of the Beatles
89 of the greatest songs from the legends of Liverpool, including: All You Need Is Love • And I Love Her • The Fool on the Hill • Got to Get You into My Life • Here, There, and Everywhere • Let It Be • Norwegian Wood • Something • Ticket to Ride • and more.

00847217	Flute	$9.95
00847218	Clarinet	$9.95
00847219	Alto Sax	$9.95
00847220	Trumpet	$9.95
00847221	Trombone	$9.95

Broadway Showstoppers
47 incredible selections from over 25 shows. Songs include: All I Ask of You • Cabaret • Camelot • Climb Ev'ry Mountain • Comedy Tonight • Don't Cry for Me Argentina • Hello, Dolly! • I Dreamed a Dream • Maria • Memory • Oklahoma! • Seventy-Six Trombones • and many more!

08721339	Flute	$6.95
08721340	Bb Clarinet	$6.95
08721341	Eb Alto Sax	$6.95
08721342	Bb Trumpet/Bb Tenor Sax	$6.95
08721343	Trombone (Bass Clef Instruments)	$6.95

Choice Jazz Standards
30 songs, including: All the Things You Are • A Foggy Day • The Girl From Ipanema • Just in Time • My Funny Valentine • Quiet Nights of Quiet Stars • Smoke Gets in Your Eyes • Watch What Happens • and many more.

00850276	Flute	$5.95
00850275	Clarinet	$5.95
00850274	Alto Sax	$5.95
00850273	Trumpet	$5.95
00850272	Trombone	$5.95

Classic Rock & Roll
31 songs, including: Blue Suede Shoes • Blueberry Hill • Dream Lover • I Want to Hold Your Hand • The Shoop Shoop Song • Surfin' U.S.A. • and many others.

00850248	Flute	$5.95
00850249	Clarinet	$5.95
00850250	Alto Sax	$5.95
00850251	Trumpet	$5.95
00850252	Trombone	$5.95

FOR MORE INFORMATION, SEE YOUR LOCAL MUSIC DEALER, OR WRITE TO:

HAL•LEONARD CORPORATION
7777 W. BLUEMOUND RD. P.O. BOX 13819 MILWAUKEE, WI 53213

Prices, contents, and availability subject to change without notice.
Disney characters and artwork © The Walt Disney Company.

The Definitive Jazz Collection
88 songs, including: Ain't Misbehavin' • All the Things You Are • Birdland • Body and Soul • A Foggy Day • Girl From Ipanema • Love for Sale • Mercy, Mercy, Mercy • Moonlight in Vermont • Night and Day • Skylark • Stormy Weather • and more.

08721673	Flute	$9.95
08721674	Clarinet	$9.95
08721675	Alto Sax	$9.95
08721676	Trumpet	$9.95
08721677	Trombone	$9.95

Definitive Rock 'n' Roll Collection
95 classics, including: Barbara Ann • Blue Suede Shoes • Blueberry Hill • Duke of Earl • Earth Angel • Gloria • The Lion Sleeps Tonight • Louie, Louie • My Boyfriend's Back • Rock Around the Clock • Stand by Me • The Twist • Wild Thing • and more!

00847207	Flute	$9.95
00847208	Clarinet	$9.95
00847209	Alto Sax	$9.95
00847210	Trumpet	$9.95
00847211	Trombone	$9.95

Disney's The Lion King
5 fun solos for students from Disney's blockbuster. Includes: Can You Feel the Love Tonight • Circle of Life • Hakuna Matata • I Just Can't Wait to Be King • Be Prepared.

00849949	Flute	$5.95
00849950	Clarinet	$5.95
00849951	Alto Sax	$5.95
00849952	Trumpet	$5.95
00849953	Trombone	$5.95
00849955	Piano Accompaniment	$9.95
00849003	Easy Violin	$5.95
00849004	Viola	$5.95
00849005	Cello	$5.95

Best of Andrew Lloyd Webber
26 of his best, including: All I Ask of You • Close Every Door • Don't Cry for Me Argentina • I Don't Know How to Love Him • Love Changes Everything • Memory • and more.

00849939	Flute	$6.95
00849940	Clarinet	$6.95
00849941	Trumpet	$6.95
00849942	Alto Sax	$6.95
00849943	Trombone	$6.95
00849015	Violin	$6.95

BOOK/CD PLAY-ALONG PACKS

Band Jam
Book/CD Packs
12 band favorites complete with accompaniment CD, including: Born to Be Wild • Get Ready for This • I Got You (I Feel Good) • Rock & Roll - Part II (The Hey Song) • Twist and Shout • We Will Rock You • Wild Thing • Y.M.C.A • and more.

00841232	Flute	$10.95
00841233	Clarinet	$10.95
00841234	Alto Sax	$10.95
00841235	Trumpet	$10.95
00841236	Horn	$10.95
00841237	Trombone	$10.95
00841238	Violin	$10.95

Favorite Movie Themes
Book/CD Packs
13 themes, including: An American Symphony • Braveheart - Main Title • Chariots of Fire • Forrest Gump - Main Title • Theme from Jurrasic Park • Mission: Impossible Theme • and more.

00841166	Flute	$10.95
00841167	Clarinet	$10.95
00841168	Trumpet/Tenor Sax	$10.95
00841169	Alto Sax	$10.95
00841170	Trombone	$10.95
00841171	French Horn	$10.95

Hymns for the Master
Book/CD Packs
15 inspirational favorites, including: All, Hail the Power of Jesus' Name • Amazing Grace • Crown Him With Many Crowns • Joyful, Joyful We Adore Thee • This Is My Father's World • When I Survey the Wondrous Cross • and more.

00841136	Flute	$12.95
00841137	Clarinet	$12.95
00841138	Alto Sax	$12.95
00841139	Trumpet	$12.95
00841140	Trombone	$12.95

My Heart Will Go On
Instrumental Solo Book/CD Pack
This arrangement of Celine Dion's mega-hit features a solo part for instrumentalists to play with a real orchestral background that sounds exactly like the original!

00841308	Solo for Flute, Clarinet, Alto Sax, Tenor Sax, Trumpet, Horn or Trombone	$6.95
00841309	Solo for Violin, Viola or Cello	$6.95